The Painted Desert

LAND OF LIGHT AND SHADOW

WRITTEN BY
ROSE HOUK

PHOTOGRAPHY BY
GEORGE H. H. HUEY

◆

PETRIFIED FOREST MUSEUM ASSOCIATION
PETRIFIED FOREST NATIONAL PARK, ARIZONA

Paperback ISBN: 978-0-945695-03-5
Hardcover ISBN: 978-0-945695-16-5

14   13   12   11   10   6   7   8   9   10

Printed in South Korea

Library of Congress Number 90-7085

PRODUCED BY: LATRANS BOOKS, Prescott, Arizona.
BOOK DESIGN: Christina Watkins
PROJECT COORDINATOR: Dwayne Cassidy
EDITORIAL: Linda Gregonis, Elizabeth Shaw Editorial
and Publishing Services.
SPECIAL CREDITS: Page 8—map, Deborah Reade; page 10—
points, Kenneth Rozen; pages 12–13—Homolovi ceramics,
Kelley Ann Hays, courtesy Arizona Archeological and
Historical Society; page 20—etching, courtesy Northern
Arizona University Special Collections; page 22—photo
courtesy National Park Service; page 23—photo courtesy
MNA; page 28—photo courtesy Navajo County Historical
Society; page 29—photo courtesy Lowell Observatory;
pages 36–37—geologic diagram, Deborah Reade; page
42—photo courtesy American Museum of Natural History;
page 45—photo courtesy MNA; page 46—illustration,
Pamela Lunge, courtesy MNA; page 54—etching courtesy
NAU Special Collections.

All photographs by George H.H. Huey unless otherwise
credited.

All photographs reproduced in this book were made on
Fuji film.

Camera and lenses: Pentax 67 System, and Fuji G617.

ACKNOWLEDGMENTS

I thank the Petrified Forest Museum Association for
undertaking this book. Their director, Dwayne Cassidy, has
been a constant source of support and friendship, and his
assistant Marian Elson, loaned me her straw hat at a most
opportune moment. National Park Service staff at Petrified
Forest, especially former superintendent Ed Gastellum,
Terry Maze, Carl Bowman, Dan Ward, and John Williams,
were cooperative at every step. Robert Long's information
on paleontological history is liberally incorporated here.

Many others assisted me in many ways. My gratitude
to Chuck Adams, Jim Babbitt, Karen Berggren, George
Billingsley, Charlie Hardy, John Hoogland, Grace Irby, Anne
Trinkle Jones, George Lubick, Scott Madsen, Mike Morales,
Barbara Phillips, Peter Pilles, Robert Preston, Irene
Silentman, Scott Thybony, Sue Wells, and the staff at the
Special Collections Library at Northern Arizona University
Library. Linda Gregonis made the manuscript far more
readable with her copyediting.

I would also like to thank designer Christina
Watkins and photographer George Huey of Latrans Books,
whose confidence drew me into this project and whose
talents shine through on every page of this book.

And I thank my husband, Michael Collier. He has
shared with me a special way to see the land he loves
so much.

COVER: Typical view of the Chinle Formation on a stormy
day in the Painted Desert. PHOTO BY T. SCOTT WILLIAMS

TITLE PAGE: Four-winged saltbush seedling.

CONTENTS

THE LAY OF THE LAND

A visitor once asked me while I was working as a park ranger at the Grand Canyon where he should go to see the Painted Desert. I paused and thought for more than a moment. That was a difficult question, I realized, because the Painted Desert is a big amorphous place. It is subtle and not easily pinpointed.

To answer his question, I pointed to the map in front of me, where the words P A I N T E D D E S E R T sprawled over a large expanse north of Interstate 40 and east of U.S. Highway 89. Though most people think of the Painted Desert as the northern part of Petrified Forest National Park near Holbrook, Arizona, the letters on the map actually described a much broader area.

The Painted Desert is a crescent-shaped arc, beginning north of Cameron, swinging southeast to just beyond Petrified Forest, with the Little Colorado and Puerco rivers cradling the southern and western edges. To the northeast it rises into the flat tablelands of Moenkopi Plateau and the Hopi Mesas.

This description may seem to indicate that the Painted Desert is a well-accepted geographic entity. Such is not the case. In researching this book, I conducted a personal poll of friends and neighbors. "Is this the Painted Desert?" I asked my husband as we gazed south from Tuba City one late afternoon. "I think it is," I said. He didn't. I asked a number of geologists, feeling certain they could offer a clear-cut distinction based on the presence of certain kinds of rock. None agreed exactly on where the boundaries should be drawn. I finally thought I had arrived when a geological field trip guide stated in no uncertain terms that mile marker 470 on Highway 89 was the "beginning of Painted Desert, characterized by peculiar and picturesque greenish, yellowish, and purplish hillocks eroded in the Chinle Formation."

Out the car window I saw on the horizon only a grayish, washed-out line of cliffs. Midmorning. No color, little relief. Indeed, depending upon the time of day, you can be in the middle of the Painted Desert and not know you are there. The reality of this place seems to be as much a function of light and shadow as it is of any topographic or geologic boundaries.

In my continuing quest, I asked an elderly Hopi woman at her home in Old Oraibi where we could go to see sunset over the Painted Desert. She looked to the ground and thought very hard for a long while, then waved her arm and said all she knew of was the place down by Holbrook, where road signs lead visitors to overlooks. Where people stare out at the desolate hills and wonder why someone started but never finished this landscape.

I defer especially to one man who attempted to define the area. Harold Colton, founder of the Museum of Northern Arizona in Flagstaff, spent a great deal of his life in the Painted Desert and in 1932 wrote a delightful little guidebook called *Days in the Painted Desert and the San*

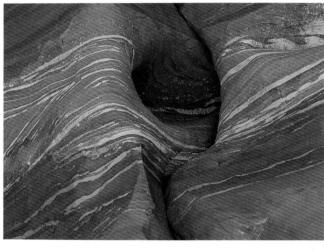

Francisco Mountains. Here are Dr. Colton's words: "Because these rocks are highly colored and the land is a treeless, grassy steppe, these wide breezy spaces have been called the Painted Desert. The name Painted Desert, then, applies to the valley of the Little Colorado, from the neighborhood of Holbrook to the Grand Canyon."

Rainfall is another standard we can use to measure this desert. Eight inches or less a year is the average precipitation in most parts, a good fit with the geographer's definition of desert as any land that receives ten inches or less a year. The Mogollon Rim, the major east-west escarpment rising south of Petrified Forest, acts as a mountain range, getting first dibs on water from any storms that enter Arizona from the south. In the "rain shadow" of the Rim lies the Painted Desert.

Moenave sandstone, yucca, and paintbrush—parts of the "desolate landscape" of the Painted Desert.

A tantalizing hint of rain hovers in May and June in the form of fluffy cumulus clouds. But all they usually bring are "ghost rains" or "virga," dark ragged curtains of water that mostly evaporate before reaching the ground. The monsoon season starts in earnest in Arizona during July, bringing what the Navajos call "male rains." Big pink-bellied afternoon clouds swell in the sky, reflecting the red earth beneath them, roaring over the hills, and casting shadows like big ink blots. In July, August, and September, the Painted Desert knows storms whose thunder shakes the ground, and whose rains fill the usually dry creekbeds bank to bank with a muddy red froth, twisting across the flat desert valleys like giant sidewinders.

It may come as a surprise to some that the Painted Desert can turn into a white, featureless, impenetrable expanse in winter. Most of this desert is above 4,500 feet in elevation, and in winter it can be as cold and bleak a place as you will ever wish not to be. Then the land and the sky are sealed together in a seamless whole.

The wind here is a force to be reckoned with. It strums your nerves and becomes your nemesis. The aridity of the desert is aggravated by the continual drying effects of the strong southwesterly winds. Wind accounts for an unestimated amount of erosion of the terrain as well. Sandstorms are not uncommon, coloring the air a diabolical yellow or dirty red and blotting out all but the closest land features. Dust devils, omens of angry gods, send cyclonic swirls of sand high into the sky.

Scientists with the United States Geological Survey started taking wind velocity measurements in the Painted Desert in 1975, but their efforts were deterred when their instruments became clogged with sand. The Desert Winds Project now uses satellites and remote monitoring stations, one of which is located atop the cliffs east of Cameron. During an early spring storm there in 1981, wind speeds were clocked at a steady forty miles an hour, gusting to sixty miles an hour—almost hurricane force— for nearly six straight hours.

Perhaps the wind has kept people from venturing too far, for among North American deserts the Painted Desert remains a relatively unstudied and little known area. Few books about deserts even mention its existence. If they do, it is treated as a stepchild of the Great Basin, one of the four great North American drylands. Botanists consider the Painted Desert an outlier of the Great Basin because of the plant life they hold in common.

In such a sparsely vegetated region, an individual twisted juniper can take on the stature of a landmark.

Plants, however, are few and far between here. Vegetation maps officially show the Painted Desert as "barren land" because greenery conceals less than five percent of the surface. Shrubs only large enough to shade a jackrabbit, and grasses, make up most of the ground cover. The plants are so distinctive and widely spaced that one individual—an oddly twisted juniper or an especially fragrant wildflower—can take on the stature of a landmark.

In addition to some living biological curiosities, the Painted Desert is a veritable outdoor museum of fossilized treasures. Great stores of petrified wood have made it famous, and in places the ground is littered with chips of these 225-million-year-old trees glittering in the sunlight. Chunks of logs split into huge rounds repose in the Black Forest of the Painted Desert wilderness in Petrified Forest National Park. The region has been known to scientists since the early part of the century for other fossils as well. The Triassic-aged rock has turned out to be a time capsule, holding everything from clams, to dinosaurs, to giant cycads, with exciting new discoveries being made almost yearly. The remains trace a revolution in life on earth—when reptiles gained supremacy and modern forms of mammals, flowers, and birds were poised on future's threshold.

The rock that offers up a great deal of this wealth is the Chinle Formation—a rainbow of pinks and reds and oranges and whites and browns and blues and grays and greens that has given the Painted Desert its name. One sunstruck scribe avowed in a 1942 newspaper article that "investigators claim they have counted 168 distinct colors and shades in the sands of the Painted Desert, and to any beholder this seems conservative, rather than an exaggeration."

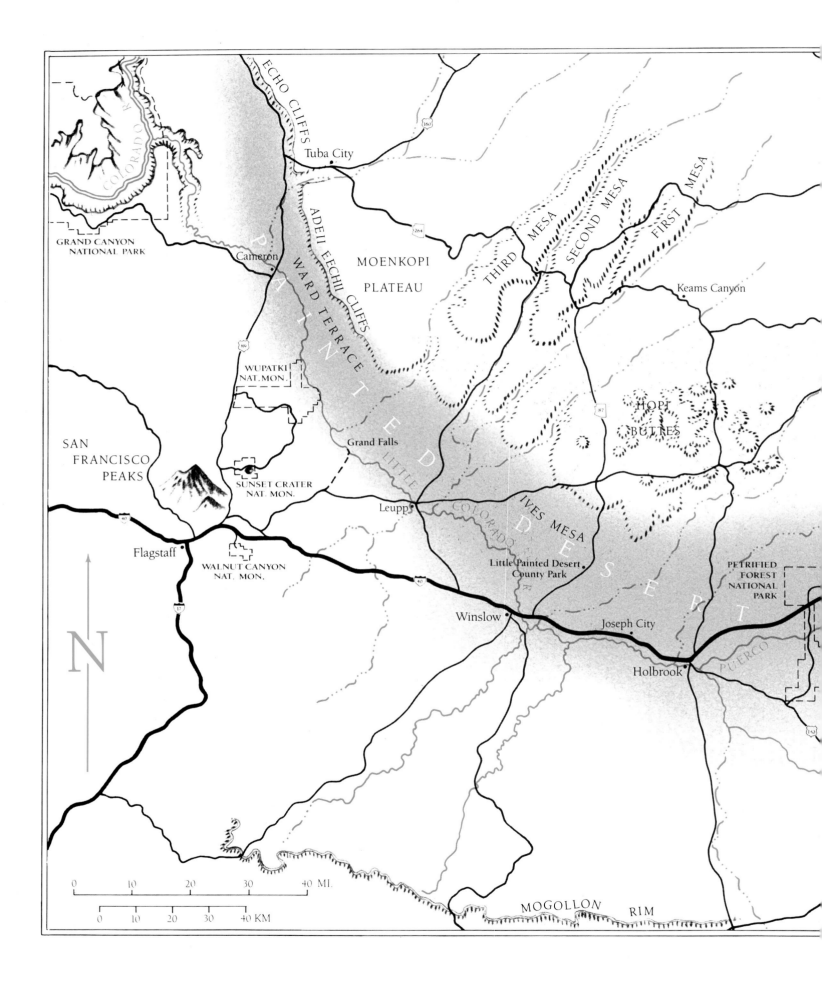

GRAND CANYON
NATIONAL PARK

ECHO CLIFFS

Tuba City

ADEII EECHII CLIFFS

MOENKOPI
PLATEAU

THIRD MESA

SECOND MESA

FIRST MESA

Keams Canyon

Cameron

WARD TERRACE

P A I N T E D

SAN
FRANCISCO
PEAKS

WUPATKI
NAT. MON.

Grand Falls

HOPI
BUTTES

LITTLE

SUNSET CRATER
NAT. MON.

Leupp

COLORADO

IVES MESA

D E S E R T

PETRIFIED
FOREST
NATIONAL
PARK

Flagstaff

WALNUT CANYON
NAT. MON.

Little Painted Desert
County Park

Winslow

Joseph City

Holbrook

PUERCO

N

MOGOLLON   RIM

0   10   20   30   40 MI.

0   10   20   30   40 KM

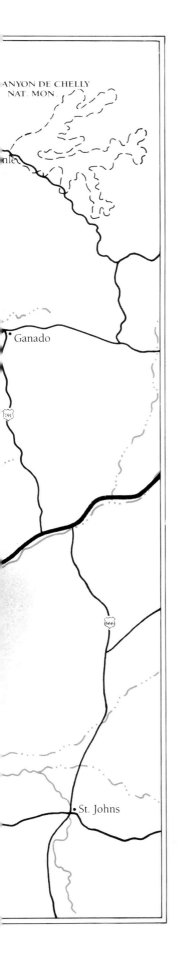

Seen from the seat of an old Cessna, 7,000 feet in the air, the colorful Chinle is an abstraction: hundreds of square miles of crenulated, tie-dyed velvet with nothing to offer perspective. The land looks soft and inviting, but on the ground that smoothness proves a deception. Small rocks perch on individual pedestals of softer dirt, just waiting to sweep your feet out from under you. Even the slightest wetting of the surface creates a gooey muck.

One of the best ways to get to know the Painted Desert is to walk in it. First realize that there's no such thing here as a straight line. I learned this one day after a park ranger advised me simply to follow a fenceline to arrive at my destination. After a half hour of scrambling up and down steep hills, dead-ending in gullies, and crawling back and forth under the fence, I laughed at myself for taking his instructions too literally. Trails and roads are foreign concepts in the Painted Desert. This is some of the most remote, inaccessible, and lonely country left on the planet. Those who enter should expect to be sandblasted by the constant wind, baked by unmitigated sun, and parched by an almost absolute lack of water. But those who venture forth adequately prepared will find a fascinating, frighteningly beautiful wild land, where every excursion is a treasure hunt.

Midway through my hike that day, I hunkered down in the lee of a big boulder. I was thirsty and the soles of my feet burned in my boots. It was only March but already the heat was severe. A raven squawked and gurgled, patrolling what I took to be a nest hidden among the cliffs in front of me. Everything around me was dry and coarse and rough. Never would I luxuriate in lushness here, but I realized too how elemental my needs were: a rock for a backrest, a piece of shade only a little larger than my body, a canteen of lukewarm water, with a raven for a companion. I realized too that I was only nibbling at the edge of this huge and seemingly unknowable landscape, but I was beginning to learn, ever so slowly and clumsily, something of the essence of the Painted Desert.

HUNTERS, FARMERS, & NOMADS

May 27. My notes show that I started into the Painted Desert from Kachina Point around sunset. The wind had blown mercilessly all day, and my only wish was to find a place out of the wind, throw down my sleeping bag, and watch night creep up over the desert.

As the sun eased lower in the sky, the reds and oranges and blues in the hills softened and deepened. I reached my destination, a special rock I remembered from a previous walk. On the boulder's patinated surface were etched figures that would be my companions for the night, some sign that humans had at one time inhabited this place.

That people actually survived for any length of time in this marginal environment is an amazement. But they have lived in—or at least passed through—the Painted Desert for a very long time. Evidence shows the presence of big-game hunters possibly as far back as 10,000 to 12,000 years ago. Over the ensuing millennia people began to settle down, establish households, grow food, and trade with their neighbors. Only three areas of the Painted Desert have been surveyed to any extent— Petrified Forest National Park, the Hopi Buttes on the northern edge of the Painted Desert, and Homol'ovi near Winslow. But in those places archaeologists have recorded hundreds of sites, from pithouses to pueblos, quarry sites, shrines, ceremonial centers, and rock art, with stone tools, pottery, basketry, and signs of agriculture giving proof of the people's lifestyle and economy.

Traces of the big-game hunters, or Paleo-Indians, amount to a handful of projectile points found in Petrified Forest and along the Little Colorado River. Migrating down the North American continent in the wake of melting glaciers, these people sought large mammals for food, such as bison and the now-extinct mammoths. Attached to the hunters' throwing sticks were sharp points of flaked stone. They carried with them blanks in kits so they could simply stop and chip out a few new points as the need arose. No doubt long hours of practice were required to become deft at this task, which some craftsmen raised to a sort of artform. Some of the recovered points are broken—perhaps discards from an artisan's imperfect attempts. Beyond these meager clues, we know little more about these people's presence in the Painted Desert.

The ensuing period, the Archaic, is represented by a few more points fashioned from the abundant petrified wood, some choppers and scrapers, and stone slabs and hearths. These are interpreted as the remains of campsites of people out hunting animals and gathering plants. From a hearth in Petrified Forest a charred piece of juniper, some Indian ricegrass, and kernels of corn were analyzed and dated. The dates indicate that the remains could have been a late Archaic site, and the early date on the corn—150 B.C.—suggests that cultivated plants were grown here about 500 years earlier than previously thought.

Next came the Basketmaker period, characterized by people who lived in pithouses located on mesa tops and river terraces. Pithouses were literally shallow holes dug into the ground, lined with slabs of sandstone and covered with poles and brush. Certainly the people of this period were living off the land—eating a lot of cottontail rabbits, deer, and antelope meat, along with seeds and nuts. Corncobs have been recovered at some sites, however, signs that agriculture was becoming more firmly established. Despite their name, these people were also making pottery. At first their ceramics were a distinctive brown type tempered with a locally available mineral called selenite, but as time went on more variety was introduced.

Few sites of the Pueblo I period, from about A.D. 800 to 950, have

Petroglyphs pecked into the varnished surfaces of boulders are tantalizing hints of the people who lived in the Painted Desert during prehistoric times. Along with stone tools (ABOVE), they are tangible remains of human habitation in this hard land.

Abandoned rooms at Homolovi are silent reminders of past people. Hundreds of residents dwelt here, overlooking the Little Colorado River. They decorated their pottery with elaborate figures called katsinas (BELOW), now central figures in present-day Hopi culture.

been found in the region. For some reason people seemed to have avoided the area then, perhaps living elsewhere, or moving closer to major rivers because of drought. Around A.D. 950, this part of the Southwest saw a sudden population explosion. More than 200 sites from the Pueblo II period, which dates from about 950 to about 1100, have been recorded in Petrified Forest alone, including pithouses, small pueblos, and ceremonial structures called kivas. Though the inhabitants began to enlarge their dwellings beyond single rooms, they still had not started to build large pueblos. The presence of small "field houses" near the dwellings suggests that more land was being farmed.

A notably different type of structure began to appear around 1075 to 1125. These so-called great kivas, larger versions of earlier kivas, likely were designed as centers where people from several settlements assembled to celebrate the harvest or other important seasonal and religious events. At the end of this time, population peaked at Hopi Buttes and continued to grow at Homol'ovi.

Then by A.D. 1250, almost as suddenly as the population had increased, it declined drastically. At Petrified Forest only one large pueblo, Puerco Ruin, was occupied. In the Hopi Buttes a single site of the period, a one-room shrine on top of an inaccessible butte, has been found. Climatic evidence suggests there was a "great drought" from 1275 to 1300, but archaeologist Anne Trinkle Jones does not believe this can explain everything. She points out that population decline began before and continued after the drought. The problem, she says, was most likely the unpredictability of the climate, and the inability of the social structure to overcome that critical factor.

In contrast, Homol'ovi, on the southern edge of the Painted Desert, was booming. There were six pueblos, some with hundreds of rooms, strung along both sides of the Little Colorado River. The one- to two-mile-wide floodplain, a better-watered area, was more suited to accommodate the people who were arriving from all directions.

In Hopi legend Homol'ovi, "Place of the Mounds," was one of the last stops for clans migrating across the Painted Desert to their present villages on First, Second, and Third mesas sixty miles to the north. They believe that the abandoned ruins are like footprints, visible to the creator so that he will know the boundaries of Hopi territory. Homol'ovi, now protected as a state park, provides a significant link between prehistoric and historic pueblo people. Hopi clan elders still return to the ruins to leave prayer feathers for the spirits of the "old people long ago," the *hisatsinom*.

Archaeologists often must deal only with the dry lifeless remains of past cultures—a potsherd here, a stone point there. But one aspect of archaeology in the Painted Desert breathes life into the science. It is the rock art left behind by prehistoric people, and by all measures the Painted Desert region possesses some of the richest examples in the Southwest. Hundreds of sites have been recorded of images mainly pecked, sometimes painted, on rock faces.

What these intriguing designs represent is a matter rife with interpretation among amateurs and professionals alike. Perhaps they were simply the erstwhile doodlings of someone bored with life. But their careful execution and subject matter seem to say more. Bear tracks, herons, antelope, snakes, lizards, spiders, human figures, and hand prints are all common in the rock art, along with concentric circles, spirals, zigzags, and dots. Not surprisingly, rock art panels are frequently found near rivers and washes, which have always been places to linger in the Painted Desert.

A fanciful petroglyph and broken pieces of pottery (BELOW) speak of a culture that devoted time to artistic endeavors, despite the day-to-day job of ekeing a living out of their desert home.

One couple has studied this rock art in great detail. Physicist Robert Preston and his wife Ann have combed the area looking for what are called archaeoastronomy sites. After many seasons of searching and observation, Robert has concluded that "funny things happen at the edges and centers" of concentric circles at summer and winter solstices. The Prestons have become convinced that prehistoric people used these solar markers as calendars and timepieces, and a growing body of evidence from throughout the Southwest tends to support them. At 6 A.M. on June 22, a day after the official summer solstice, I stood with Bob Preston and a few others in a "cave" of overhanging boulders and watched as a point of sunlight touched the exact center of a circle and then began to retreat. This was only one of many such examples the Prestons have discovered. Another, at Puerco Ruin in Petrified Forest, is watched closely each morning during the week bordering the summer solstice. Visitors can observe a shaft of sunlight illuminating a spiral on a sandstone boulder, a convincing demonstration that these ancient people were perhaps more sophisticated than we might at first suppose.

These sorts of discoveries only add to the fascination and mystery of the Painted Desert. It is a place where we can ponder entire cultures—from Ice Age big-game hunters to the modern-day Hopi and Navajo—people who learned to live in this lean land long before we arrived. A place where we can add significant dimension to our own lives and perspectives of time.

◆

The creation story of the Navajo Indians explains how this high desert country, which is their home, was made. It all began as the gods were trying to get rid of the giants and monsters that roamed freely about the world. Changing Woman, *Asdzą́ą́ nádleeh*, was given five colored hoops. The black one she rolled to the east, the blue one to the south, the yellow one to the west, and the white one to the north. The fifth, multicolored hoop was thrown into the sky to the high-noon sun, along with five colored knives.

Changing Woman watched as clouds gathered from the four directions. The sky turned an eerie orange, and thunder shook the earth. The storm lasted four days and four nights. On the fifth day the weather cleared, but only briefly. Violent whirlwinds then began to blow, threatening to destroy her house. To ease his mother's fears, her son Monster Slayer made four blankets of clouds and fog and fastened them over their house.

"El desierto pintado" north of Winslow. The Navajo creation story tells how Changing Woman created the colors of the high desert country that is now the Navajo Reservation.

Finally, after four more days of hail and winds, the people emerged to a clearing sky. Monster Slayer threw the coverings off the house, along with the rainbows, sunbeams, and lightning he had used to fasten them to the ground. The sky was filled with bright sparkling colors, and the people saw that their mountains and grasslands had turned into pillars of naked rock and cliffs of red and yellow. Changing Woman and her people were satisfied that surely now the alien giants had been destroyed.

In fact, the nomadic Navajos were not the first people in this part of the Southwest. Though the time of their actual arrival remains a point of debate among archaeologists and historians, they may have started south from the Bering Sea area only a thousand years ago. The Navajo definitely were living in New Mexico by the time the Spaniards arrived in the sixteenth century. For a while the Navajo coexisted with the Pueblo people more or less harmoniously. But the *Diné*, as the Navajos call themselves, started to raise livestock (brought originally by the Spaniards), and to live in dispersed settlements, thus expanding their territory and surrounding the Pueblos.

The United States Army arrived in 1846 and became a force that

would change the history of the Navajos forever. In 1863 and 1864 the army, under General James Carleton, forcibly moved the Navajos to Bosque Redondo (Fort Sumner) in New Mexico, in what is now known as the "Long Walk." In the 1870s, after the Navajos had returned from their exile, they began to settle in the Little Colorado River valley. In 1900 and 1901 nearly two million acres were added to the reservation, most of it in the Painted Desert.

Some Navajos still live here in the traditional way—in circular hogans, herding livestock, making jewelry, and weaving fine rugs. Though this is the driest part of their reservation, some farming also is practiced. Small corn patches struggle in the sandy hills and wash bottoms, relying on seasonal rains for survival. In other places, irrigation is in use. Near Leupp, about fifty miles east of Flagstaff on the Little Colorado River, a project called Navajo Family Farms uses Israeli drip irrigation techniques on forty acres of vegetables. Since 1984 the award-winning venture has raised food for more than 500 people.

The San Francisco Peaks are a constant presence on the horizon as one journeys in the Painted Desert. The Peaks guided early explorers and are held sacred by both the Hopi and the Navajo.

From the Painted Desert, Navajos have always enjoyed a view of one of their four sacred mountains, *Dook'o'oosliíd*, the San Francisco Peaks. The Peaks, says Navajo George Blueyes, are "adorned with abalone" and "these mountains and the land between them are the only things that keep us strong." The Hopi too believe the San Francisco Peaks, *Neuvatikyao*, are sacred. Their summit is called "cloud house," the place where the spiritual beings called kachinas live for part of the year.

I awoke one morning in the Painted Desert, shoulders stiff from sleeping on the hard ground. The first sight that met my eyes was the San Francisco Peaks, their elegant sweep gracing the horizon to the west. I would see them often from many directions during my Painted Desert explorations, and they became an anchor not only to the landscape but to me. Gleaming snow caps them in spring, green in summer, gold in autumn, then again in winter they become "adorned with abalone." I began to understand why these mountains are sacred to so many.

EXPLORERS

The San Francisco Peaks served as a landmark for many other, earlier Painted Desert explorers. The Spaniards, among them Coronado's expedition in 1540 and Espejo in 1583, passed through the region in search of wealth. Though they never laid claim to the coveted seven cities of gold, they left their heritage in the form of names on the land. The environs of Cameron, Arizona, were once known as the Melgosa Desert, for Captain Pablo de Melgosa who accompanied Coronado; Garces and Tovar mesas are situated in the center of the Painted Desert; and the Spaniards reportedly called the colorful land east of the Peaks *el desierto pintado*.

Four hundred years after the Spanish explorers left the area, surveyors working for the U.S. Army came west to chart possible routes for transcontinental railroads. Like the Spaniards, the military men depended upon the Hopi and Navajo for crucial information and guidance, while at the same time carrying out their onerous mission of ridding the West of the so-called "Indian problem." By this time a few mountain men and trappers knew the country intimately too, men like Antoine Leroux, who acted as scout for several expeditions.

Among the first of the army men to pass through was Captain Lorenzo Sitgreaves. In 1851 he led an expedition along the Zuni and Colorado rivers, following the Thirty-fifth Parallel. By October they had reached the Painted Desert region. Sitgreaves included in his journal frequent observations on the soils and rocks they encountered. Near Petrified Forest he noted that the ground was "strewed with pebbles of agate, jasper, and chalcedony, and masses of what appeared to have been

The Black Forest within Petrified Forest National Park well fits Captain Lorenzo Sitgreaves' description of what he saw in 1851. The ground, he said, is "strewed with pebbles of agate, jasper, and chalcedony, and masses of what appeared to have been stumps of trees."

stumps of trees petrified into jasper, beautifully striped with bright shades of red . . . blue, white, and yellow."

The only place they could find wood and water was along the Little Colorado River, so they plodded down it, crossing and recrossing, assiduously trying to avoid the quicksand, mud, and sloughs. Upon reaching Grand Falls, about forty miles downstream from present-day Winslow, Sitgreaves decided to turn west toward the San Francisco volcanic field after his guides informed him that the river continued through an impassibly steep canyon to the confluence with the main Colorado.

(OVERLEAF)
In December 1853 the Whipple expedition encountered a creek that they called "Lithodendron" for the stone trees that littered the region. Lithodendron Wash cuts across the Painted Desert in the north part of Petrified Forest National Park.

Two years later, under the lead of topographical engineer Amiel Weeks Whipple, the first wagon trains entered the region. Accompanying the engineers were geologists, zoologists, botanists, meteorologists, astronomers, artists, and even the occasional writer. Their voluminous reports, maps, and artwork have become historical classics that contain invaluable baseline information about the unknown lands they traversed.

Nineteenth-century scientific surveys bore little resemblance to those of today, except perhaps in the small size of their budgets. The Whipple party, with $150,000 in government money, equipped itself as a small mobile convention. Present were nearly a hundred scientists, engineers, soldiers, and teamsters, thirteen wagons, two carts, and a menagerie of mules, cattle, and sheep. During their December travels across northern Arizona, they endured stampeding mules, sand that sucked their wagon wheels down to the hubs, and the deadly scourge of smallpox that was epidemic among the Indians of the region.

On December 2 Whipple reached a large stream that snakes across a good part of the eastern Painted Desert. Lithodendron Wash was Whipple's name for the watercourse, signifying the abundance of "stone trees" he saw. The men had discovered that day "Quite a forest of petrified trees . . . prostrate and partly buried," including one that was ten feet in diameter.

Those discoveries were matched by a reputed abundance of grass and water. Whipple remarked that even with two hundred mules, cattle, and sheep, grass was plentiful for all. Here, he insisted, "nature has furnished grass, sufficient water, and a climate most favorable" for livestock raising. Baldwin Möllhausen, the stocky, bewhiskered Prussian artist-in-residence with Whipple, offered a somewhat contradictory view. When they pitched their tents for the first time on the Little Colorado he said the grass in the valley was "yellow and withered" and only short, scattered tufts of grama grass grew on the hillsides. Had they known what lay before them, however, they would have considered these the Elysian fields. "Often enough afterwards," wrote Möllhausen, "we should have esteemed ourselves most happy to fall in even with such pastures."

Möllhausen was also along on a later expedition, this time in 1858 with Lieutenant Joseph Christmas Ives, steamboating up the lower reaches of the Colorado River and riding overland on mules across northern Arizona. Also accompanying Ives was John S. Newberry, a renaissance man who served not only as geologist but also as medical doctor for the expedition. Newberry is credited as the individual who first officially affixed the name Painted Desert to the eastern side of the Little Colorado River valley.

In early May Ives and his men had passed the San Francisco Peaks and descended to the Little Colorado. It had been a rough trip. Sudden snowstorms, scarce and sometimes nonexistent food and water, and the difficult terrain had reduced their mules to a sorry state. "They look and move like slightly animated skeletons," the lieutenant wrote. The expedition's provisions were nearly gone and their packs were torn to shreds, yet Ives was determined to see the country to the northeast.

The Little Colorado River was swollen with spring runoff, requiring them to call into service a Buchanan boat, an "admirable invention" of canvas lashed to a portable wooden frame that could be assembled in about ten minutes. Ives, foreseeing the possible need of such a craft, had one especially made for the overland part of his expedition. Once assembled, it was eleven feet long, five feet wide, and two feet deep, and weighed 150 pounds. They loaded aboard, pulled the boat across the river by their pack straps, and let the mules swim. The expedition was now split in two. Ives, Newberry, and eleven others waved goodbye to their friends on the opposite bank and headed northeast across the valley.

Reaching the top of some bluffs above the river, Ives described a scene "of utter desolation. Not a tree nor a shrub broke its monotony. The edges of the mesas were flaming red, and the sand threw back the sun's rays in a yellow glare. Every object looked hot and dry and dreary." It was here that Newberry applied the English translation of the Spanish "el desierto pintado," the Painted Desert. To him this name well described the area's barrenness as well as the colorful reds, blues, greens, oranges, purples, browns, lilacs, and yellows of the rocks.

The men continued for another desperate fifteen miles, though their mules were flagging badly. "The country, if possible, grew worse," Ives wrote, and he made up his mind to return to the river the next day and search for an Indian trail. As the sun began to set, Ives' mood improved. The "condemned region," he said, proved not entirely devoid of life as scorpions, spiders, rattlesnakes, and centipedes emerged "to enjoy the evening air."

They located the Indian trail, a well-traveled path that took them due north. Luring them on was a line of "beautiful blue peaks [that] stood like watch-towers" in the distance. These were the Hopi Buttes, the striking volcanic remnants that jut above the flat plain and mark the general northern boundary of the Painted Desert.

As Lieutenant Joseph Christmas Ives crossed the western Painted Desert, the Blue Peaks (now called the Hopi Buttes) rose up in front of him "like ships approached at sea" (ABOVE). So despairing were Ives and his men of the barren desert that they might have failed to appreciate its finer points, such as the lovely purple flowers of locoweed (BELOW). Ives' name went to a colorful, eroded mesa (OPPOSITE) in the Painted Desert north of Winslow.

VISITORS

It was Amiel Weeks Whipple, rather than Joseph Christmas Ives, who charted the route that would be followed by the Atlantic and Pacific Railroad. The Thirty-Fifth Parallel, the route of Whipple's survey, follows the valleys of the Puerco and Little Colorado rivers from New Mexico into Arizona. The A&P strayed little from that line, completing track-laying across northern Arizona in the winter of 1881-82. The railroad's contribution was commemorated by naming the towns of Holbrook and Winslow after railroad owners and engineers. Near Holbrook, turn-of-the-century train travelers could disembark and stay at the Adamana Hotel and be guided through the renowned wonders of the Petrified Forest.

By the 1930s, Highway 66, that famous vagabond road, also followed this transportation corridor. For the Painted Desert region the road commenced a "new era," according to Charles "White Mountain" Smith, custodian of then-Petrified Forest National Monument. Tourists had ready access to the land north of the monument, by then known as "the Painted Desert," and local residents thought this a natural addition to the monument. Smith recommended in May 1932 that the monument's boundaries be extended as soon as possible to incorporate this northern 53,000 acres.

The Painted Desert Inn afforded early travelers to Arizona a memorable view of the Painted Desert in Petrified Forest National Park. The Inn is now a National Landmark.

"White Mountain" Smith had recently returned from an eighteen-mile drive through the area with Herbert Lore, proprietor of the Painted Desert Inn perched on the edge of Kachina Point. The inn was a popular stop, and Mr. Lore stowed a Model A at the base of the foot trail so that in dry weather he could escort visitors on a two-hour drive through the desert. A special attraction was the Black Forest, of great scientific interest because of the abundant dark petrified trees it contained, and unfortunately of great interest to visitors who could not resist picking up free samples of the wood as souvenirs. The Black Forest, Onyx Bridge (a 55-foot-long petrified log spanning a gully), Chinde Mesa, and Pilot Rock were all good reasons for the government to acquire the acreage. Roger Toll, on detail from the National Park Service, said he knew of no other part of the so-called Painted Desert where the coloring was as brilliant as in the proposed addition. Four months after Smith made his recommendation, the Painted Desert section was added to the monument.

Visitation figures proved this to be a wise move. By 1936 the government began spending money to drill a well, refurbish the Painted Desert Inn, and improve the five-mile Painted Desert Rim Drive. The twenty-eight-room inn, with its pueblo revival architecture, became a favorite place from which to view the dramatic panorama of the Painted Desert that stretched to the horizon.

The inn, a harbor for cross-country travelers for decades, was closed during World War II. It reopened in 1946, and in 1948 architect Mary Jane Colter hired Hopi artist Fred Kabotie to paint murals on the walls. One of Mr. Kabotie's scenes depicts the Hopi walk across the Painted Desert to the Zuni Salt Lake to gather salt.

In 1961 the inn was closed again. The building's foundation began to crumble and the roof leaked, and visitors could only peer through darkened windows at the famous Kabotie murals. Another temporary reopening, for the nation's bicentennial in 1976, sparked renewed interest in saving the building. In 1988 the Painted Desert Inn was designated a national landmark, and the Park Service began renovating the building for eventual use as a museum.

Perhaps "White Mountain" Smith would now say that yet another era has commenced for the Painted Desert. In 1970 it was designated the first official wilderness in the national park system. Places earn this designation for their outstanding solitude and lack of human presence, places "untrammeled by man." Visitors may now enter this wilderness only on foot or on horseback. It is a worthwhile venture, if even for a day. To wander amid the hills is like walking in a Georgia O'Keeffe painting. But to do so unprepared could mean serious consequences. Water is the utmost requirement because there is almost none to be found in this desert, save for a few ephemeral pools. A topographic map and the ability to read it is the second prerequisite. Notifying park rangers of your plans is the third. What is necessary to remember is that the wilderness makes no value judgments, and has no sympathies or capacity for forgiveness.

At hearings on the Painted Desert wilderness, one Park Service representative spoke of the special character of this wilderness: "a character of openness and the hint of loneliness. . . . The nature of the terrain has the effect of telescoping distance, with the result that a day's walk for a man, say twenty miles, is measured by the eye as a minor span, against the immensity of the total view."

Yesterday, as today, visitors to the Painted Desert were awed and inspired by the dramatic landscape.

RIVER OF FLAX

One evening I sat on a cutbank of the Little Colorado River at the mouth of a large sandy wash, watching a skein of birds migrating up the river channel. They broke ranks from their V formation, weaving back and forth like the tail of a kite. Their silence and the dusky light did not permit positive identification. Geese perhaps, or possibly cranes.

The birds were silhouetted against the western sky, the clouds lit softly in shades of peach and apricot and orange. Time they were stopping for the night, but instead they continued northward, following the river. As dusk descended, the water in the river changed from a molten copper to quicksilver. Water, I thought, mocks the word "desert."

The Little Colorado River. Colorado Chiquito, the diminutive child of the mother Colorado into which it flows. On old maps it was Rio de Linum, or River of Flax, possibly for the straw-colored water and sand. To the Hopi Indians it is *Paayu*, "river," and to the Navajos *Tooh*, "large body of water." A newer generation has simply shortened it to the familiar "LC." Hardly a great river by many standards, the Little Colorado is an Eden to all living creatures of the Painted Desert.

Dried stems of sacaton grass. (BELOW) The Little Colorado River—The River of Flax.

Near the source on Mount Baldy in the White Mountains of east-central Arizona, the Little Colorado is a pleasant, gurgling trout stream. As it flows northwestward from these origins, the river lazes out into a flat, sandy streambed refreshed with water only during spring snowmelt and the summer monsoons. Then it becomes a silty, reddish brown soup which, according to the old bullwhackers, was "thick enough with mud to make good adobe." In raging flood, the Little Colorado can support impressive quantities of water. Eighteen thousand cubic feet a second would be a high flow, but during a good part of this century average runoff has reached only about 250 cubic feet a second, barely enough to float a small boat.

The contributors to this rich brew drain an elliptical-shaped basin of 15,840 square miles. From the Painted Desert enter the major tributaries of the Puerco River, and Lithodendron, Leroux, Cottonwood, Oraibi, Polacca, Jadito, and Dinnebito washes, their arms etched like the branches of a tree over the land. In their beds are swirls of marbled sand and mudcracks that look like curled rawhide. Because they are dry most of the time, these washes form convenient avenues for travel across the Painted Desert.

The Little Colorado serves both as passageway—and barrier —to people trying to make their way through the vast expanse of the Painted Desert. The river's quivering quicksand is legendary and, in the days before bridges, at only a few places such as Sunset Crossing near Winslow,

(OVERLEAF)
Several times a year runoff swells Grand Falls on the Little Colorado River.

Tanner's Crossing near Cameron, and Black Falls did bedrock provide firm enough ground for fording.

Just before the bridge at Cameron was completed in 1911, Sharlot Hall met the Little Colorado. Miss Hall, Arizona's first territorial historian, had embarked on a wagon trip to the Arizona Strip country in the northwest corner of the state. She knew one of the biggest obstacles between her and her destination was the Little Colorado.

Descending from the pine forests of Flagstaff on July 23, 1911, Sharlot Hall recorded her first sight of the Painted Desert. "The whole region," she wrote, "is a tangle of sandstone cliffs and ridges burned and eroded into the most fantastic shapes by wind and blowing sand." As hoped, she and her guide encountered the Lee's Ferry Mining Company, a group of men with eight or ten wagons and Texas cattle, freighting machinery to a placer gold operation at the ferry on the "big" Colorado a hundred miles to the north. When they arrived at the banks of the Little Colorado, a sandstorm was howling and water was running "in a big sheet of silver to the river." With the help of the mining crew, they forded at Tanner's Crossing without incident. Things might look different to Miss Hall now. Except for a few samples of historic or prehistoric graffiti on the rocks, that once-famous crossing has fallen into disuse, a spot no longer marked on the ground or on many maps.

Another crossing, which has not been lost in obscurity, is Grand Falls. This "Niagara" of the Southwest, about thirty-five miles east of Flagstaff, is a popular destination in spring and late summer. Grand Falls is not shown on every map, but can be reached on an "improved" road of washboard gravel. A low line of tamarisk trees unceremoniously announces the Little Colorado, but the falls can't be seen until you walk to the edge. Assuming you are there when the river is flowing, you will see a two-tiered, 185-foot drop roaring with caramel-colored water. On the west bank, you will notice black columns of rock, vestiges of the creation of this spectacle. This tongue of basalt spewed from a crater in the San Francisco volcanic field, damming the Little Colorado and forcing it to cut a new channel. As rivers will, the Little Colorado worked around the lava flow and back into its old canyon. To get there, it had to drop back to its former level—hence Grand Falls. Harold Colton advised that "After a period of heavy rain, the falls are at their best. Then is the time to make your visit."

We traveled to Grand Falls one evening in March. It hadn't rained, but snow was melting fast in the White Mountains that year and the Little Colorado was flowing early. As we approached the brink, I felt the spray on my face being blown out of the gorge before I actually saw the falls. The Hopi know Grand Falls as "swishing/whistling sound place." Their visits to this place may have been spurred by the plentiful supply of polished cottonwood root that collects in the slack water at the base of the falls, raw material for their carved kachina dolls.

Grand Falls was also well-known to a group of people who came down the Little Colorado more than hundred years ago. In 1876 leader

Brigham Young called the Mormons to build homes and farms in the central Little Colorado Valley and to "make acquaintance with the Indians and do them good."

A reconnaissance company had traveled from Utah three years earlier to survey conditions there, and their news was not good. Leader Horton Haight reported that the Little Colorado River was "a Small amount of Salty Mineral water and quicksand and mineral bottom." He went on to describe sand-choked roads, poor feed, and bad water. Another member of the company was even less complimentary: this was "no fit place for a human to dwell upon. . . . The most desert lukkin place that ever I saw, Amen."

But a heavy dose of faith can move people as well as mountains. In January 1876 the call came and 200 people set out from Utah to the valley of the Little Colorado. The Arizona Mission, under the leadership of Lot Smith, William C. Allen, Jess Ballenger, and George Lake, founded four settlements along the river—Joseph City, Obed, Brigham City, and Sunset. Their route through Arizona was across the Colorado River at Lee's Ferry, south to Bitter Springs, Limestone Tanks, Willow Springs, Moenkopi, Black Falls, and Grand Falls on the Little Colorado, and then to the settlement sites. They immediately set about to find building timber and water fit for drinking, but their primary task was to establish an irrigation system.

Four days after their March arrival, the Latter-Day Saints began to build a dam on the Little Colorado at Joseph City and what was then Obed. On July 19 the dam was washed out in a flood. Every year for the next eighteen years the settlers chose a new location for another dam, and spent long hours and most of their money rebuilding the dams and lengthening the irrigation ditches. They were learning the hard way of the nature of a fickle desert river.

Finally, in 1894 they mastered the river with a dam at Joseph City that stood for the next twenty-nine years. By that time Joseph City was the only one of the four original settlements that remained. As historian George S. Tanner has written, "The wonder is not that a large majority of the settlers became discouraged and deserted the mission, but that any remained."

In 1876, Mormons from Utah traveled to settle the valley of the Little Colorado in Arizona. Historian George S. Tanner wrote "The wonder is not that a large majority of the settlers became discouraged and deserted the mission, but that any remained."

A group of history buffs in Winslow did not want the story of the pioneers and their monumental struggle to be lost, so they staged a re-creation of the passage along the "Mormon Trail." In March 1976, on the hundredth anniversary of the trip, they followed the route from Lee's Ferry to Winslow on horseback. For the next five years they repeated the ride, thirty miles a day for five and a half days, with a pickup truck meeting them along the way with soda pop and meals.

Among the loyal riders was Charlie Hardy, who is always happy to take curious people along the faint trail that heads north from his home in Winslow. We went out with him one day by modern conveyance, in "Max," a friend's four-wheel-drive vehicle. Charlie took us out across the scrublands to see the monument of petrified wood that marks the site of Brigham City. I asked Charlie why they chose this location. "Because nobody else wanted it," he replied.

A group of Flagstaffians, circa 1917, returning from the Hopi Reservation, ford the Little Colorado River.

We traveled on to Tucker Flat, a dry bowl of red clay that becomes a lake in wet years. This had not been a wet year, in fact the West was deep in drought and the desert was as dry as chalk. Not much in the way of flowers this spring, I allowed. Said Charlie in laconic response: "If it'd rain every Saturday night, we'd see all kinds of things blooming out here." The only green we could see was the line of cottonwoods marking the course of the Little Colorado in front of us.

From Tucker Flat we followed the road to Tucker Spring, one of those rare places in the Painted Desert where travelers could get a drink of fresh water. "Live water" they call it, a precious commodity in this land of bitter springs and salty wells. As a kid, Charlie said he would hike to the spring with a sandwich and would always bring back a Mason jar filled with the delicious water. The year-round spring, flowing from sandstone at the top of a hill, has run at its present plentiful level for as long as Charlie can remember.

This Mormon Trail, of which there are several in this part of the West, was also called the Honeymoon Trail. According to Charlie, betrothed couples would leave the valley in the fall and travel by wagon to St. George in southwest Utah, where they could be properly wed in a Saints' temple.

We finally reached the boundary of the Navajo Reservation where a locked gate forced us to turn around and head back. A fine red dust clogged my nostrils and coated my skin and clothing. It was high noon, and smoky mirages shimmered along the banks of the Little Colorado, mirages that have fooled desert travelers for a long time.

As the Mormons so painfully learned, the Little Colorado is an unruly old stream. They might have benefited from information that scientists have accumulated about the river in this century. Geologist Richard Hereford has looked at the stream's behavior from 1900 until the 1980s and has documented constant shifts in the river as it adjusts to changes in climate and other factors such as land use. Hereford's studies show that from 1900 to around 1940 the Little Colorado's channel was eroding. Big floods cut a wide sandy swath largely devoid of plants of any kind. That ended in the 1940s and early 1950s as annual rainfall decreased. Floods weren't as frequent, annual discharge was about half the preceding level, and the channel's width was reduced. Plants like tamarisk trees gained a foothold and spread along the dry riverbed. The years from 1952 to 1978 were wetter, flows again increased, and the floodplain started to build.

Those changes in plant life have interested botanists as well as geologists. The older channel of the Little Colorado is marked by a stand of native Fremont cottonwoods, the "alamos" described by the early explorers. Tree-ring studies show that these trees sprouted between 1800 and 1905, and they once lined the banks of the river.

Vegetation along the banks now is dominated by tamarisk, an exotic

The Rio Puerco, a tributary of the Little Colorado, is an intermittent stream that rages with frothy, mud-laden water in summer flashflood. Even intermittent flows provide enough moisture for cottonwood and tamarisk trees along the river's edge.

species. Tamarisk (or salt cedar) is called an exotic not for its feathery, plumed branches, but because it is an introduced plant from the Mediter-ranean region. This shrubby Old World tree was first documented along the Little Colorado near Winslow in 1909. Since then, "tammies" have spread wildly along any watercourse they can find. Their tiny, abundant seeds (one strong plant can produce fifty million seeds a year) are carried by the wind and can sink down a tap root within twenty hours of hitting good ground. Tamarisk competes with native plants for water and creates a different habitat for birds and other animals that live along the river.

Another exotic plant that has overgrown the floodplain is camelthorn. Though its pretty pink flowers lend a pleasant color to the landscape in summer, camelthorn is a nasty nuisance that knows no bounds.

Over the camelthorn flats lining the Little Colorado, marsh hawks cruise, looking for any rodent that makes a false move. Birds that can live nowhere else in the desert, such as the prehistoric-looking great blue heron, can be seen along the river. Toads, which require water to complete their life cycle, set up a howling chorus at night from the slimy river mud that is their home.

As I thought about this desert river, for some reason a conversation I had a few years back echoed in my mind. I was riding on a boat near Sitka, Alaska, watching whales and bald eagles. A fine rain had started to fall. I was talking with a Tlingit Indian woman who I had just met, and we were telling each other of our homes.

When I said I lived in the desert, she shook her head. She had spent her life on the coast of southeast Alaska, and to her desert was obviously a foreign place and idea. "I must be part water," she said, and smiled. If she is part water, I thought, then I must be part sand and rock. Yet I understood what she meant about water. For desert dwellers, water is not so much a fact as a determiner of life. It tethers us, and all other living things, as tightly as any leash. It is as much gift as essence of life. I was reminded too of a story of a Navajo woman who, when crossing the bridge over the Little Colorado River at Cameron, threw out a pinch of corn pollen and said: "So there will always be enough water for everyone."

HALCHÍÍTAH

Navajos call the Painted Desert *halchíítah*, "amidst the colors." The lovely hues of blue and purple, white and gray, pink and red, are the country's trademark. One rock in particular, the Chinle Formation, is largely responsible for creating this pastel palette. Back in 1917 geologist Herbert Gregory proposed the name Chinle for exposures of the rock in the valley of Chinle Wash up near Canyon de Chelly. Though Gregory's rock is what geologists call a "type section," the Chinle actually crops out over a large part of northern Arizona, southern Utah, western New Mexico, and southwest Colorado. Some of its most fantastic exposures are in Petrified Forest National Park.

The mudstones of the Chinle Formation exhibit various colors. Here the blue and gray bands indicate a different rate of oxidation of the minerals. (OPPOSITE) Reds and pinks and oranges speak of a higher degree of oxidation. The rocks, literally, have rusted.

The Chinle reminds me of the multicolored layer cake I always asked my mom to bake on my birthday. The Chinle's layers are mudstones and sandstones, and the variegated colors are attributed to mineral content and the different rates at which the sediments were laid down. When the sediments were being deposited slowly, soils had time to develop. Oxides of iron, aluminum, and manganese became concentrated in the soil, and these concentrations gave rise to the breathtaking reds and purples in the northern part of Petrified Forest. The blues and grays and greens in other parts of the Chinle resulted from reduction, in which oxygen was removed from the environment, just the opposite of what happens in oxidation.

The mudstones that make up most of the Chinle are clay—the finest particles produced by rock decay. The Chinle is rich in an especially absorptive clay called bentonite, formed from decomposed and altered volcanic ash. Under a microscope, bentonite is a chemical sandwich of alternating sheets of water and aluminum and silicon-bearing groups. Everyone knows—or soon will if they walk or drive in it—that the Chinle becomes slippery when wet. The layers of water surrounding the wet clay particles cause this slipperiness. If you walk on Chinle that is the slightest bit moist, you will also find that it turns into a sticky goo. Globs of the stuff will bind quickly to the soles of your shoes, adding a few pounds to every step you take. When wet, bentonite can swell to seven or eight times its dry volume. When it dries, it shrinks. This constant, spongelike action

gives the Chinle those characteristic stretch marks, a texture much like elephant skin.

The source of the volcanic ash that accumulated to form the thousand-foot-thick deposits of Chinle remains a matter of great speculation among geologists. Ash from volcanoes can be blown hundreds, even thousands, of miles from the actual site of an eruption. Witness a volcano of recent history, Krakatoa in Indonesia, which blew in 1883. Smoke and ash from Krakatoa fogged skies for months over the western United States, and explained the brilliant sunsets seen during December of

Strange erosion patterns mark the Chinle Formation (ABOVE AND OPPOSITE). The high bentonite content means that Chinle shrinks and swells as it is alternately wet and .dried, giving rise to the cracks and nubbly texture of the surface.

that year. Two hundred and twenty-five million years ago, when the Chinle sediments were being deposited, an upland volcanic area called the Mogollon Highlands probably existed somewhere to the south and west. These elusive mountains are widely believed to be the contributors of the ash that washed into northern Arizona to become solidified as the Chinle Formation.

The other big question is what the climate and environment were like during Chinle times. Was it tropical? Subtropical? Or even arid? Again, examination of the Chinle clays has led sedimentologists to conclude that climate may have alternated between humid and dry. But paleobotanists, looking at ancient plant fossils, find little evidence of an arid climate. There is general agreement, though, that Arizona was much closer to the equator then, and that the ocean was in western Nevada. Arizona would have been a coastal plain, with large, slow-moving streams flowing northward across a broad lowland. These streams carried the eroded ash—the mud and silt— that would be transformed into the coat of many colors we now feast our eyes upon in the Painted Desert.

One morning a man stood at an overlook in Petrified Forest and insisted to his wife that the colors had washed away since he was here fifteen years ago. Maybe he was right. The Chinle does erode at a remarkable rate. One of the most vivid examples I have seen is in the Little Painted Desert County Park north of Winslow. A trail consisting of railroad ties bolted into the ground marches bravely down the hillside. Some well-meaning soul wanted to encourage people to get out of their cars and experience the Painted Desert on a more intimate level. But the Chinle is winning. In places big hunks of the hill have slumped off, and water has burrowed large holes under the ties. Other ties have been put in place to create quick detours around the undermined sections.

Back in the 1950s, Dr. Edwin Colbert of the Museum of Northern Arizona tried a more scientific experiment to measure the Chinle's rate of erosion. He poked stakes into the ground and went back each year to measure how far the surface had receded. After ten years, he found that the average amount of erosion each year on steep slopes is a quarter of an inch, on gentler slopes half that amount. This means that the Chinle badlands are losing one to two feet of surface every century! All the

necessary ingredients are present for this amazing destruction—soft rock, dry climate with occasional torrents of rain, and little or no plant cover.

Some other odd effects of erosion of the Chinle are pipes and sinkholes. Once water finds a way into a small crack in the mudstone, it trickles down and enlarges the crack into a hole that emerges at the base of the hill; other times the holes become cavelike openings large enough for a person to crawl into. One must step cautiously over these hills lest he fall into the bowels of the Chinle.

The Chinle has a partial defense against these onslaughts of weather.

In many flatter places it is protected by a covering of desert pavement, pebbles and rocks consisting mostly of fossils and chert, and an occasional large, very old granite or quartzite cobble that might have come from the "basement" of the Mogollon Highlands. Each stone, in a cradle of sand, looks like it has been individually placed by some giant hand. At certain times of day, the sun catches the angles on the rock and they glitter like pieces of broken mirror over the ground.

This armor of small stones on deserts nearly everywhere has attracted geologists' attention. What causes it, they wonder? The standard explanation is that desert pavement results from wind blowing away the smaller pieces of sand and dust and leaving only the larger pebbles on top. Others think the rocks have actually levitated, or risen from below, to accumulate on the surface. As one geologist puts it, the pebbles are "up on jacks" of sand and clay. Still a third explanation has the rock there from the beginning, and it is then broken apart by repeated freezing and thawing and shrinking and swelling of the ground. Whatever the cause, this

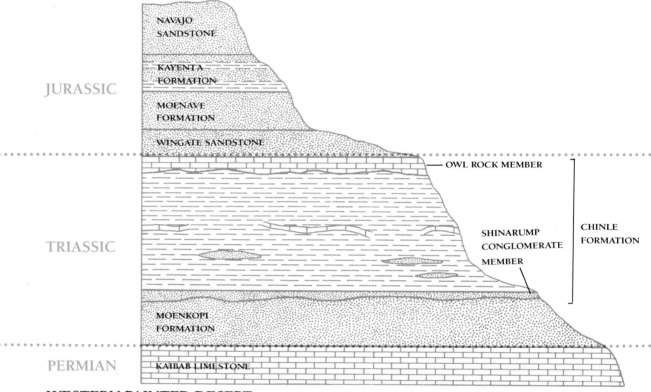

WESTERN PAINTED DESERT

"pavement" provides a mantle of protection from further erosion if left undisturbed. But once the coarser stones are gone, wind and water can go about their business, carrying away the finer underlying particles.

◆

The Chinle Formation has been divided into several "members" or parts, subject to different names depending upon which geologist is doing the lumping or the splitting. For now, though, the lion's share of multicolored rock is called the Petrified Forest Member. Above that is the younger Owl Rock Member, atop Chinde Mesa and on Ward Terrace east of Cameron. The Owl Rock is mudstone and thin limestones deposited in shallow bodies of water, and fossils it contains might help explain climate changes that may have been occurring during those days. Below the Petrified Forest Member is the uranium-bearing Shinarump Member.

Though some geologists would define the Painted Desert strictly on the presence of the Chinle Formation, others would include the rock formations above and below as well, not only because they appear in the valley of the Little Colorado but because they assuredly add to the meaning of *halchíítah*. On either side of Highway 89 going north toward Cameron you can see the bright redbeds of the Moenkopi Formation, which underlies the Chinle. The Moenkopi is 600 to 700 feet of brick red shales and sandstones thick with salt and gypsum. Gypsum—hydrous calcium sulphate—is a soft white rock called an evaporite, which forms when crystals precipitate out of evaporating seawater. Usually this reaction occurs in a very dry climate, so the abundance of gypsum (and salt) in the Painted Desert indicates extreme aridity at certain times when the rock was being born.

Cliffs retreat in the distance east of Highway 89, each rising progressively higher—Ward Terrace, the Red Rock Cliffs, and the farthest

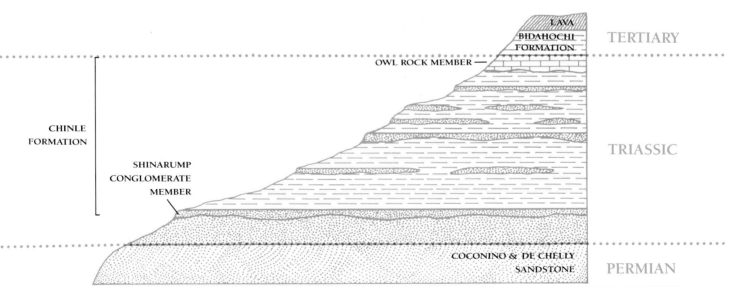

EASTERN PAINTED DESERT

and highest, the Adeii Eechii Cliffs. Though they appear devoid of features from a distance, a closeup view reveals a landscape of gargoyles and hobgoblins. They erode into buttes, mesas, ledges, cliffs, knobs, and pillars. These escarpments are infinitely dissected, with canyon after canyon heading up into them. The silence is deafening, and the trill of a rock wren is a major event. A stock tank, the foundation of an old stone hogan, or an occasional cow are the only signs that people live in this land.

The cliffs consist of layered rock that rests on top of the Chinle, formations that show a marked change from the Chinle days of streams and lakes to a time when nearly two-thirds of the Colorado Plateau was a desert not unlike today's Sahara. Elegant sweeps of crossbeds in the sandstones tell the various directions of the wind as it blew over these drylands.

This classic southwestern sequence of sedimentary rocks includes, from bottom to top, Wingate Sandstone, Moenave Formation ("silty sandstone and sandy siltstone"), Kayenta Formation (mostly purple shale and sandstone), and Navajo Sandstone, a white sandstone capping the Adeii Eechii Cliffs. The Navajo is permeable to water, and from its base emerge springs that have served people in this region for a very long time—Tuba City is built near one, the small settlements of Willow Springs and Moenave at others.

This sequence of rocks vanishes as you move southeast across the Painted Desert, having been eroded and removed from the area. In Petrified Forest and in the Hopi Buttes area a different and younger rock rests on top of the Chinle. It is the Bidahochi, the "forgotten formation" of the Painted Desert. A lack of color—it is mostly black and yellowish-gray—has left the Bidahochi pretty much ignored. But the formation tells us a great deal about some fairly dramatic events of more recent geologic time. The Bidahochi is much younger than the Chinle, deposited in a shallow basin during the last twelve million years or so. In Petrified Forest you can see exposures along the first four miles of the Painted Desert Rim Drive and under Pilot Rock in the northwest corner of the park. The Hopi Buttes, which provide the northern backdrop for the larger Painted Desert area, are another excellent place to see this formation.

Wind, a significant erosional force in the Painted Desert, creates a sandstorm in the Adeii Eechii Cliffs. Desert adapted plants, such as the prickly pear (ABOVE), take advantage of pockets of sandy soil.

The Bidahochi consists of two distinct parts; one is made of silt, sand, and mud deposited in a lake, the other is the result of volcanism. What geologists think happened is that the flows of certain rivers, including the ancestor of the Little Colorado, were disturbed as the Colorado Plateau was being uplifted. Streams slowed down, ponds and lakes formed, and loads of sand and silt were deposited in the valley. One gigantic lake, called "Hopi Lake," was some 7,500 square miles in size. The lower part of the Bidahochi is made up of the sediments deposited in this lake. Then volcanoes began to erupt in these lakes, with lava welling up through fissures in the sediments. The hot rock cooled quickly in the water into rounded lumps called "pillow lavas."

The lava along the Painted Desert Rim Drive erupted about 300 yards east of Pintado Point. This is a pale reminder of the hot times to the north in the Hopi Buttes volcanic field, where nearly a hundred separate volcanic remnants rise from the plain, adorned with beautifully sculpted basalt columns. These dark monoliths are called diatremes, pipes through which

molten rock traveled to reach the surface. Early geologists, such as J. S. Newberry, called them the "Trap Buttes," the word "trap" referring to the volcanic rock. Four to eight million years ago the Hopi Buttes area must have resembled a Pittsburgh steel mill—steamy, noisy eruptions hurled large blocks of volcanic rock into the air. Today certain of these buttes are sacred to the Navajo and Hopi, for their spires are the homes of golden eagles, whose feathers are used in ceremonies.

The other major geologic feature of the Painted Desert—sand

Moonrise over Ward Terrace in the western Painted Desert.

dunes—is the most ephemeral. George Billingsley of the U.S. Geological Survey produced a beautiful map of the southern Ward Terrace area in 1987. In only a few years, he says, the map has become out of date because the sand dunes shown on it are no longer there. As sand dunes will, they have packed up and moved on. One fascinating revelation of Billingsley's work is that these dunes are actually part of a giant recycling system: The cliffs crumble and the bits of sand are carried southwesterly downstream when the washes are running. Then, during dry times, that famous Painted

Desert wind picks up sand and silt from the streambeds and blows them
northeastward back onto the higher terrain whence they came. The dunes
form ramps as they try to climb the faces of the retreating cliffs, seen from
Highway 89 in the vicinity of Cameron. Eventually some of the sand is
transported back down the washes and into the Little Colorado.

Yale geologist Matt Walton has called the Painted Desert "a landscape
of destruction." Drifting dust and violent rains eat away at the shales and
sandstones to create "a land carved into a bewildering waste of washes and

arroyos separated by knife-sharp ridges and weirdly etched mesas."
Badlands. But, he says, the Painted Desert is constantly being recreated out
of its own ruins. It never stops. Those grains of sand could conceivably be
transformed once again into a cliff of sandstone.

BONE HUNTERS

The wheels were spinning and the radiator was hissing. We were stuck. Nobody got too excited, though, because this is an expected occurrence when traveling the "roads" in the Painted Desert. We got out, ate lunch, and waited for the truck to cool down so we could continue.

I was with a group of people from the Museum of Northern Arizona headed for a place that I had wanted to see for some time. Nearby was a canyon and a wash, of which there are hundreds out here. But this particular canyon held what has been touted as one of the best dinosaur track sites in the West. This site has a long history that only added to its interest. We must go back to the early days of paleontology in this country, when the greats like Barnum Brown, Lester Ward, and Charles Camp were poking around in this part of the world. Barnum Brown, curator of vertebrate paleontology at the American Museum of Natural History in New York City, first came to the Painted Desert in the early 1900s. In 1929 a Navajo shepherd, Goldtooth Semahly, told Cameron trader Hubert Richardson about a number of large prints or tracks up a canyon about fifteen miles to the east. As soon as Brown heard of the discovery he hurried out to the Painted Desert to investigate. They went to Semahly's site in December of that year and uncovered nearly 300 tracks, all three-toed imprints anywhere from six inches to nearly sixteen inches long.

A few years later Brown's assistant-to-be, Roland T. Bird, returned to the track site for a closer look. The thirty-two-year-old Bird was tooling around the West on a motorcycle with an ingenious homemade camper as a sidecar, living off earnings from odd jobs. He stopped in at Cameron and asked about the trail to Dinosaur Canyon. "Why, boy, there's no trail to Dinosaur Canyon," Richardson told him. But Bird, fresh from Mexico, felt sure he and his trusty motorbike could negotiate anything the desert had to offer.

So he filled every water jug he had and headed east from Cameron. Dodging sand dunes and roaring up washes, Bird pushed his Harley into a land of stone gnomes. He saw faces with eyes, ears, mouths, and beards. Perhaps the sun was getting to him. He went as far as a wheeled vehicle could take him, then set off on foot. The "depressing optical effect of clear desert air" made Bird feel like he was on a treadmill, going nowhere. Finally arriving at the base of the cliff where the site supposedly was

(OPPOSITE) Near Dinosaur Canyon, east of Cameron, where Barnum Brown conducted some of his first paleontological digs in the Painted Desert.

Renowned paleontologist Barnum Brown (LEFT) pictured here with Henry Fairfield Osborn, president of the American Museum of Natural History, at a diplodocus site in Wyoming.

located, he saw spread before him a square mile of land. Barnum Brown's track site could be anywhere.

Using a photograph to guide him, Bird followed a small wash. Soon he spotted some familiar sandstone with strange markings. "I brushed away the sand. An unmistakable three-toed track! And another, and another, and another!" Eureka! Bird was lost in this land of dinosaurs for the rest of the day. Nightfall forced him to stop. He walked out to his waiting steed in darkness, ate a cold supper, and fell asleep, no doubt dreaming of hairy gnomes and giant lizards stalking the land.

Nothing much came of Bird's or Brown's work on the tracks for some time. For fifty years the site was relegated to the musty halls of scientific oblivion—until 1986 when it was rediscovered by a new generation of enthusiastic paleontologists. Scott Madsen, then with the Museum of Northern Arizona, had run across an old picture of Bird at the site; in an almost identical reenactment of Bird's experience, he studied it closely and recognized the rock formations. On a hunch he and friend Keith Becker returned to the vicinity of Dinosaur Canyon and in a couple of hours found the site again—a half-century after Bird and Brown had been there.

Upon locating a certain topographic feature, "we knew for sure we would find the tracks," Madsen wrote in a letter to Barnum Brown's daughter Frances. They were so excited they ran most of the way toward a butte, but couldn't immediately find the tracks. Then they noticed two rocks on the ground that were exactly in the same place as in the Bird photo. "We moved a few feet right of the stones and dug and brushed several inches of sand and gravel away—and there was a large 3-toed track!"

The two "laughing and grinning fools," as Madsen called himself and his companion, swept the desert floor. They spent two days working on the spectacular site. Madsen even found a valve stem from an old motorcycle tire, which he always likes to think belonged to Bird's Harley.

So here I was, stuck in the sand, but still holding hope of seeing these famous tracks that I had tried unsuccessfully once before to find. I was elated to be here with people who apparently knew where they were going. Graduate student Grace Irby had chosen the trackway site for the subject of her master's thesis. We were armed with brooms and picks and shovels, ready to help Grace uncover the tracks once more. I'm pleased to report that we actually made it.

The trackways are a rare find in the Moenave Formation, the 208-million-year-old red rock that forms the hoodoos that haunted Roland Bird. The actual site is a rock slab about fifteen by twenty-five feet, and embedded in the surface are literally hundreds of large and small, three-toed prints or tracks, some with actual claw and pad marks, leading in every direction. A big dinosaur dance floor.

I was getting a taste of the anticipation and exhilaration that all

The famous dinosaur track site near Cameron, discovered by a new generation of paleontologists in the 1980s, is covered with hundreds of three-toed tracks. The animals that left these prints roamed the area about 200 million years ago.

paleontologists must feel as they engage in their chosen profession. They set out across barren wastes, sand blowing in their eyes and ears, the sun baking their heads, searching always for another treasure. The Painted Desert is like a sunken Spanish galleon for them, for around any corner may lurk another discovery like the Brown/Bird track site, or perhaps the hardened bones of a new dinosaur, or the carbonized leaf of an ancient plant.

Lester Ward knew the feeling. So did Annie Alexander, Charles Camp, Ned Colbert, Sid Ash, Rob Long, and Michael Parrish, to name only a few. Ward, paleobotanist and social reformer, came to Arizona for the first time in 1899. He was here to study the advisability of making the area around Holbrook a national park to protect the petrified wood. During his explorations, Ward uncovered petrified bones and teeth of a large, water-dwelling reptile called a phytosaur along with a few interesting plant fossils, though not as many as he would have liked. He returned the following year with Barnum Brown and they worked the same territory, finding more fossils. Ward's bonebed near Cameron continued to yield exciting fossils into the 1950s. His presence and significant work are forever memorialized by the naming of Ward Terrace for him, the act of geologist Herbert Gregory.

Paleontologist Edwin Colbert and crew excavate a prehistoric reptile skeleton from its rock tomb.

After word of Ward and Brown's finds reached other scientists, the pace of discovery quickened, especially in the Chinle Formation of the Petrified Forest. An elderly John Muir spent time in Petrified Forest in 1905 and 1906. In his wanderings in the Black Forest he collected the first pieces of armor plates of an aetosaur, a reptile that resembled an armadillo. In 1921 Annie Alexander, heiress and founder of the Museum of Paleontology at the University of California at Berkeley, saw Muir's fossils and launched a long line of research at Petrified Forest. Impressed during a trip there, she invited twenty-eight-year-old Charles Camp to join her for the summer field season. Before Camp arrived in June, Miss Alexander and her associate Louise Kellogg had already discovered a promising fossil deposit in the Painted Desert in what is now called the Devil's Playground area—including a new phytosaur species and the first evidence of a mammal-like reptile called *Placerias*.

With Camp on the scene, the team spent the rest of June prospecting and excavating fossils. They found skulls, toothplates, limb and jaw bones, and a host of remains of various animals. The bonebeds in the park proved so rich that Camp returned year after year for nearly a decade. Most of Camp's collections are housed at the University of California at Berkeley, where he was ensconced in an office thanks to Miss Alexander's largess.

Ranger naturalist Myrl Walker continued paleontology work in Petrified Forest during the depression years, again finding outstanding specimens, even a new species, in Devil's Playground and elsewhere. After a hiatus, Dr. Edwin Colbert, then with the American Museum of Natural

History, found phytosaur remains in 1946. But his plans to continue work in the park were derailed by his momentous discovery of bones of the little dinosaur *Coelophysis* at Ghost Ranch, New Mexico.

The story of paleontology in the Painted Desert has since assumed a familiar pattern of discovery and rediscovery. Mounds of old collections were never prepared and some scientific papers never published. Consequently a new generation reopened a Pandora's box, identifying not only much of what had been found by their predecessors but also finding an incredible array of new species and forms during fieldwork in the 1970s and 1980s.

Robert Long dug into Charles Camp's collections in Berkeley, which included thousands of specimens and hundreds of pages of meticulous field notes. Camp's sites near Petrified Forest and Cameron were revisited by Long and several colleagues. In 1984 they discovered the highly publicized "Gertie" in the badlands just below Chinde Point in the Painted Desert. Gertie's limb bones were removed from her Chinle sepulcher, bound in plaster casts, and helicoptered out of the park. The remains were then sent to the laboratory at Berkeley for preparation. Gertie's specific identity remains unknown, though "she" is believed to belong to a group of medium-sized, meat-eating dinosaurs and is possibly the oldest one yet found in the region.

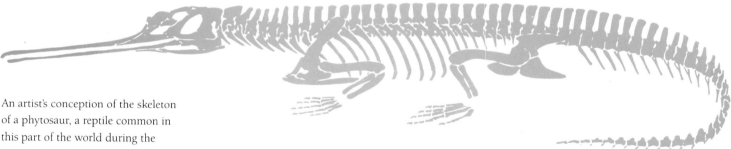

An artist's conception of the skeleton of a phytosaur, a reptile common in this part of the world during the Triassic Period.

What had caught the fancies of everyone from the late 1800s to the present were the extensive exposures of Chinle rock of Triassic age, 245 to 208 million years old. The Triassic—the beginning of the Age of Reptiles— was a time when the earth and life on it was undergoing a major revolution. Dinosaurs of all kinds roamed the Painted Desert, but they were still in their infancy. They had not yet come to dominate the planet as they would in the next two periods, the Jurassic and Cretaceous. Competing with them were bizarre-looking, Dr. Seuss-like creatures, some of them pretty big and scary. Paleontologist Dale Russell has described them with such vernacular names as cowturtles, gatorlizards, and owliguanas. But by the late Triassic, dinosaurs were on their way to a long and fruitful reign in the world.

A person traveling in the Painted Desert during these times would have witnessed a wild animal park par excellence. Fish that look much like modern ones swam in the freshwater lakes and streams, along with snails and clams; beetles and cockroaches nibbled on ferns; a stubby-bodied reptile with the face of a dog grunted from its hiding place underneath a log; a flying reptile called a pterosaur patroled the skies. Phytosaurs, with long skinny snouts and dagger teeth, were everywhere.

Fresh coyote tracks in mud on a frosty morning are sign of the ramblings of the desert song dog.

The plant life in this part of the world during the Triassic was fairly dense and luxuriant, and perhaps would have resembled the swamps of present-day south Florida. "Primitive" horsetails, the hollow-stemmed scouring rushes that grow along streams today, may have reached thirty feet in height during the Triassic. Ginkgoes, ferns, and cycads, plants that look like pineapples, added to the verdant scene.

Over them all towered straight-trunked, cone-bearing trees, some up to 200 feet high. The best-known conifer is the one that produced the bulk of the petrified wood in the Painted Desert. *Araucarioxylon arizonicum* is its scientific name, now Arizona's state fossil. When these trees died, most fell to the ground, were washed down streams, and collected in lagoons and swamps. Covered with silt, they were deprived of oxygen and their decay nearly ceased. Silica minerals then filled or actually replaced the wood cells, crystallized, and transformed the trees into jewels of quartz, jasper, and amethyst.

Paleontologists are also sweating the small stuff now. They are down to microflora and microfauna—the tiniest bones sieved out of tons of sediment, and pollen grains that require electron microscopes to see their detail.

French author Honoré de Balzac once said that paleontologists are poets who reconstruct past worlds from blanched bones. If so, the generations of paleontologists who have worked here have added many verses to the as-yet-unfinished Painted Desert poem.

LIFE IN THE BADLANDS

John Hoogland is a busy man come the end of May. When I first met him, he was literally running around—in shorts, visor, and boots—in the field behind the housing area at Petrified Forest National Park. Not only was Dr. Hoogland apparently jogging in midday in the desert, but his skin was covered with curious black splotches.

John Hoogland is a zoologist, and his specialty is prairie dogs. He was in a hurry because he was trying to mark all the emerging young dogs before they overheated in the sun. Before he let them go back into their burrows, he tagged their ears and painted each one with black hair dye (thus explaining his dark skin splotches).

Dr. Hoogland's study of Gunnison's prairie dog, the species that lives in the Four Corners region of the Southwest, involves their "kinship." To a

(OVERLEAF)
A rabbitbrush in glorious golden bloom defies the notion that there is no life in the Painted Desert.

biologist that means answering the question of "who copulates with whom," he said. In addition Dr. Hoogland wants to know whether parents recognize their kin, whether they kill each other's babies as he has observed in black-tailed prairie dogs, and how the prairie dog's alarm call relates to kinship.

Cynomys gunnisoni lives in colonies underground. Selection of sites for their "towns" is a mystery, but in this large one John estimated there were 300 to 500 adults. Sometimes the same colonies will be reinhabited year after year. In mid to late March they mate, some females with more than one male. The female is pregnant for twenty-eight or twenty-nine days. During this time she builds a nest in the burrow, where the hairless young are born, eyes closed. At five and one-half weeks, the weaned newborn dogs see the light of day, coming out of their subterranean tunnels to eat. Gunnison's prairie dogs hibernate from October to February, and as time draws nigh all employees at Petrified Forest are asked to watch for the first sign of their awakening.

Prairie dogs are, obviously, creatures of the prairies. But where is there prairie here? Nebraska, maybe, but in Arizona? Admittedly it is not true prairie, a designation reserved for the tallgrass prairie that once cloaked the heart of the Midwest. What is found here is another type, called shortgrass prairie.

Grassland is a major plant "zone" in the Painted Desert, but the lines drawn between it and the second major zone—Great Basin desertscrub—are not always distinct. The variables that affect plant growth are amazingly complicated and numerous. Thus, a look at Petrified Forest's vegetation map shows more of a mosaic of communities, and we shouldn't be too disturbed at finding a desert shrub growing alongside grasses. With that qualifier, we can look at these ecosystems individually, while keeping in mind their fuzzy boundaries.

The Painted Desert grassland can, when greened up after summer rains, bring tears to the eyes of an Iowan. With only about nine inches of rain on average a year, however, the shortgrass prairie exists here in what botanists call an "extreme tension zone." It is nearly at its farthest westward extension, and the best stands are found mostly on high mesas and plateaus that have deeper, loamier soils and that receive an inch or so more precipitation than locally lower areas.

Old-timers reminisce of the days when the grass tickled the cow's bellies. Overgrazing of the range, and severe drought, which began in 1891, brought all that to an end. In a 1977 report, researchers with the University of Arizona's Office of Arid Lands Studies recapped the history of vegetation in Petrified Forest. Upon completion of the railroad in 1882, longhorn cattle were brought in to the area by the thousands. Fortunately for the ranchers and for the land, the years 1887 through 1890 were blessed with more than enough rain. Herd sizes increased, and in 1891, just as a large calf drop occurred, the wet period screeched to a halt. Markets for the surplus cattle were as dry as the ground. With little alternative, the stock were kept on the range, "stripping it bare and churning the soil to dust."

The devastating drought persisted for two more years. By that time a million cattle had died, and range plants had been eaten to the quick. Rain returned in 1894, and the Painted Desert region turned from a dust bowl into a mud bowl. With no vegetation to secure it, topsoil washed away by the tons. During drier times, wind blew the dirt to Kansas.

Since the 1930s, most of Petrified Forest National Park's grasslands haven't felt the nibble of a cow. In testimony to the earth's capacity to heal itself, native grasses (and some non-native ones as well) have resurged. Now the rich grasslands inside the park's boundary fence stand out on satellite and aerial photos, in marked contrast to surrounding lands.

Grasses are ideally suited to dry windy places such as the Painted Desert. Silicon oxides in the outer covering of the stems keep them tough and upright, but they are still flexible enough to bend with the wind. The shallow but thick roots of shortgrass form an underground net of sod that soaks up moisture that might have drained down to deeper-rooted plants. Some grass species are especially tenacious. Perennial blue grama, the one Navajos call "bent grass" for its graceful recurved spikelet, will invade surrounding areas during drought.

The economy of the prairie is one of sharing, with homes commonly recycled among different animals. The Gunnison's prairie dog burrows, for example, might one day become the dwellings of burrowing owls. The owls will set up housekeeping in burrows, usually after prairie dogs or ground squirrels have abandoned them. Though the owls can excavate their own burrows, they tend to rely on "starts," remodeling existing burrows to their liking.

TOM BEAN

After these small gray owls migrate back to Arizona in the spring, they form pairs and males serenade the females at the burrow entrance through the night. They work together to scratch out the burrow that will hold their nest. An owl spends most of its time on the ground near a burrow or sometimes perched on a fence post, vigilantly keeping watch for skunks, badgers, coyotes, bobcats, and snakes. Insects, especially grasshoppers, make up a significant portion of their diet, though that can vary with what's in season. When burrowing owls hunt, they forage over the ground and pounce on their prey, or they hover above ground then stoop to pin down prey with their talons.

The other animal known to use prairie dog burrows is the endangered black-footed ferret. In fact, a distribution map of the black-footed ferret would neatly overlap that of the prairie dog. Biologists attribute the ferret's

A prairie dog watches with full alertness for any danger. A burrowing owl (BELOW) borrows an abandoned prairie dog home.

endangered status to control efforts against prairie dogs—the ferrets being victims through secondary poisoning, loss of potential homes, and lack of food (they eat prairie dogs). The most recently known population of these weasel-like mammals was a small group in Wyoming, but it has since become extinct. But biologists continue to search for ferrets, especially in prairie dog towns in grasslands. So far no sightings of these masked nocturnal animals have been confirmed in the Painted Desert, but wildlife biologists are looking at possible promising sites for reintroducing them elsewhere in Arizona.

Horned larks are unfailing companions in the Painted Desert. (BELOW) The wide-open grasslands of this desert well suit the swift pronghorn.

STEPHEN TRIMBLE

Another pillar of the grassland community is the horned lark. *Eremophila alpestris*—a name that means "desert-loving"—is sometimes called the prairie bird. The only lark native to North America, this pale tan, professorial-looking bird is a constant year-round companion in the Painted Desert, even when little else is moving about. A group of them will flutter up out of a shrub, or one will pick at seeds on a grass stalk, never alighting. Males lure females with their courtship songs, and nests are built of fine grass in shallow depressions in the ground. Horned larks seem able to bear the full brunt of the desert environment, inhabiting the flat, open country with little shelter from plants.

The quintessential large mammal of the prairies is the pronghorn. The two, the grassland community and the pronghorn, seem to have evolved together: the vast unbroken spaces suited to the animals' keen eyesight and running ability, their buff tan coats the color of golden grasses. At the slightest sign of danger—the sight or smell of a bobcat or coyote on the prowl—a pronghorn flips its white tail to warn others in the herd of the need to flee. These long-legged sprinters can run as fast as the wind, at speeds up to sixty miles an hour.

The pronghorn is as all-American as its prairie roots. The name "antelope" is really a misnomer and properly belongs to an Old World hoofed animal. Pronghorn have horns, not antlers. Males regularly, and females occasionally, shed their horn sheaths.

Pronghorn were once more abundant in this part of the country. In 1909 seventy-five of them were counted between Winslow and Holbrook, and another forty-one were reported near Petrified Forest. These beautiful creatures can sometimes be observed in the grassland strip that separates the northern and southern portions of Petrified Forest, eating fresh wheatgrass and needlegrass in the spring. By summer, when grasses have dried and toughened, and in winter when the grasses are dormant, they resort to shrubs such as sagebrush.

They (and some grasses as well) also possess a distinct leaf anatomy that permits a different style of photosynthesis. They are called C_4 plants, referring to the number of carbon compounds that are the first products of photosynthesis. The standard path for most plants is C_3, for three-carbon compounds, and for decades scientists thought that was the only pathway plants used. The discovery of C_4 photosynthesis by biochemists in the 1960s was fundamental and revolutionary in the botanical world. During photosynthesis in warm weather, C_4 plants can fix twice as much carbon dioxide as C_3 plants can, thus developing more sugars and enjoying faster growth. It is an adaptation that allows these plants to function in the hot, bright desert.

With moisture, the shortgrass prairie comes into its own. To see this grassland in full green is perhaps a shock to our common perception of the Painted Desert as a barren wasteland.

Four-winged saltbush earns its common name for the quartet of broad, parchment-like wings on each seed. The Latin name of the species—*canescens*—refers to the whitish scales that cover the stems and leaves of young plants. This powdery "scurf" is a defense against desert dryness, shading the plant from excess light and heat and lessening evaporation from the leaf surfaces. Young saltbush seedlings proliferate along washes in the Painted Desert, their fresh blush of pink lending a soft touch to the desert.

Four-winged saltbush conducts business with other compatible associates such as shadscale and greasewood. All three belong to the goosefoot family, a clan that has enjoyed a long and successful reign in deserts throughout the world. ("Goosefoot" refers to the shape of the leaves in many members of this family, such as the weed commonly known as lambsquarters. Also part of the family are our favorite vegetables, spinach and beets.)

These three species—four-winged saltbush, shadscale, and greasewood—are called halophytes, or salt lovers. Most plants would shrivel up and die if exposed to the concentrations of salt that these plants

endure. Halophytes are able to absorb salts and store them in special bladders that cover their leaves. Or they can secrete the salts through their pores as they transpire, or breathe. A simple test can be done to see just how salt accumulates in these plants: Touch your tongue to a seed of four-winged saltbush and you will experience a distinct salty taste.

Shadscale is the plain-Jane sister of four-winged saltbush—no ruffly seeds, only rigid spiny branches—but she may win the prize as the tougher of the two. Great Basin botanist Hugh Mozingo says that shadscale is "truly a desert plant" that can grow in the driest locations. In North

America it has a wide range, from Mexico to Montana and from California to North Dakota.

Greasewood, a real alkaline-lover, grows in low areas with internal drainage, places with the heaviest clay soils and greatest salt concentrations. The taproots of this bright evergreen shrub penetrate deeply into the soil to reach the water table. Researchers have found that greasewood seeds germinate at low temperatures, a good insurance policy that they will start life in the springtime, when conditions are more favorable to growth, rather than in summer.

Jackrabbits might have a hard time of it here without greasewood. It is a major food source for this long-eared hare of the Painted Desert, and also provides shade for the animal. Although this *is* desert, the cold winters mean fewer reptiles than in warmer climes; but a few do live here and are worthy of note. Lizards are fairly well represented —you may find the lesser earless, the eastern fence, the sagebrush, side-blotched, and short-horned. Three species of spadefoot toads and some harmless and beautiful snakes—glossy, gopher, milk, and night snakes, to name a few—are all inhabitants here and a lucky observer might be able to see one or two of them.

Overlaying these two basic communities—the grasslands and desertscrub—is a specialized habitat, the sand dunes. Some are remnants of a large sand sheet that covered the area millions of years ago. Others are produced by the weathering of sandstones, and still others come from sand blown in from streambeds. Sand dunes form separate ecosystems that present different conditions to plants and animals. Water permeates down into sand dunes and gives up moisture readily to plants. Some dunes have settled down with a family and mortgage. They are called stable dunes, made so by the number of plants that have succeeded in keeping them in place. Other dunes are active, advancing anywhere from one to eighty feet a year; they lack sufficient plant cover to hold them in place.

Sand dune plants display all sorts of special adaptations to their unique environment. They have adventitious roots that grow along the stem to provide anchorage. The narrow-leaf yucca that grows on dunes in the Painted Desert employs this strategy. Dune plants must make hay while the sun shines—or before the sand covers them—by setting seed and growing quickly. Dune plants such as the lovely Indian ricegrass have found a way to make up for the nitrogen deficiency common in their sandy homes. Their roots are covered with a sheath where nitrogen-fixing bacteria live. To withstand the light and heat of their sandy desert environment, plants such as rosemary mint and sand sagebrush have silvery leaves. Rosemary mint is a graceful soft shrub that blooms with delicate purple flowers in April. Square stems and opposite leaves are a sure sign of its membership in the mint family.

Another common dune plant, Mormon tea, has become the object of

A striped wood snake, as illustrated in the Sitgreaves Report of 1854. A black-tailed jackrabbit (BELOW) keeps cool during the heat of the day in the shade of a shrub.

study in Petrified Forest for its interesting biology. It is found in sandy places throughout the Southwest, and earned its name from the fact that early settlers brewed a tea of the green branches. What has attracted botanists to the plant is its questionable heritage. This member of the joint-fir family may be a link between the two major groups of plants on earth today—the angiosperms and the gymnosperms. Angiosperms, or flowering plants, have seeds enclosed in an ovary. Gymnosperms, with naked seeds, include the conifers and ferns, "lower" plants that were around long before angiosperms. Mormon tea bears small structures that first look like cones but then develop into what look like inconspicuous flowers. Its reproductive processes also appear to be a hybrid of both groups. By determining the characteristics Mormon tea has in common with flowering plants, researchers may be able to answer questions of how flowering plants evolved.

Sand dunes cast a veneer over the Painted Desert, constantly on the move, presenting challenges to plants that try to colonize them.

Wandering up a wash one day, my nose caught a scent that said "desert" to me. I looked around and didn't see any large tree or flower that might be sending off such a delicious aroma. Then I sharpened my eyes a little more, and noticed a flurry of yellow along the edge of the wash. It was a shrub covered with sweet yellow flowers, whose fragrance had not only attracted me but also swarms of tiny insects the exact lemon-yellow color as the flowers. The plant had cleverly lured these insects in; they were sipping the sugary nectar in the blossoms, but at the same time were unwittingly performing yeoman service as pollinators of the plant. I was thrilled when I was able to find the shrub in a book at home. It is called, obviously enough, dune broom. But beyond its mere identification, the shrub-insect interaction illustrated the remarkable intertwinings of life in this desert.

If the Painted Desert looks barren to you, look again, or try to return in spring. Some 337 species of plants have been counted in Petrified Forest National Park alone. In March, April, and May, after a wet winter, the desert is transformed into a garden of wildflowers: Sand dunes host the tissue-thin flowers of evening primrose, swaying in the wind on their thin stems, their delicacy in stark contrast to the rough surroundings. The intoxicating sand verbena, an annual dune flower, appears in April, and by May the solitary mariposa lilies have come on the stage. Autumn displays its own colors, with golden rabbitbrush and chartreuse globes of wild buckwheat lining the roadsides, and clumps of purple asters gathered at their feet.

Though wildlife is not often apparent in the Painted Desert, an evening or morning walk among the dunes and washes will reveal some sign of animals. Black Pinacate beetles come out in the evening, walking purposefully over a dune with their head bowed to the ground in supplication. The "runways" crisscrossing dune fields on any morning indicate the frenetic nightlife of kangaroo rats and mice. These secrets of the Painted Desert—the small but momentous discoveries—require patience. They are what will bring me back again and again, what will help me someday begin to know the seemingly unknowable.

APPARITIONS

Evening primroses and purple asters (BELOW) flaunt their delicate beauty in this forbidding desert. Their very presence is a wonder and a gift.

Chinde Point, on the rim of the Painted Desert in Petrified Forest, takes its name from the Navajo word for "spirit." Everywhere in this land are apparitions, people and things that appear unexpectedly. Perhaps these spirits are contained in the rock art, the squiggles and swirls the ancients made to tell them when the sun had completed its journey across the sky in summer. Perhaps they rest in the Sipapu, near the mouth of the Little Colorado River, where the Hopi emerged from the underworld, or in the stone foundations of an old Navajo hogan. Perhaps they are manifested in falling stars that streak across the endless, black night sky, or in the startled daytime stirrings of an owl. Or perhaps a single chip of petrified wood, concentrating the pastel colors of the surrounding rock, may be the keeper of the spirit of the Painted Desert.

In the end then, it may not be so important to worry about the specific boundaries of this entity called the Painted Desert. What is important is to spend some time with and in it, learning the history of the people, the other animals, and the plants that give it that elusive sense of place.